To Paige,
You are
Hope you love it

Hearts and Souls

Of Special Olympics.

Ruth Spinelli and Alean Skinner

Publisher

CHECKMATE PRESS
checkmatepress.com

McLean Media Group, LLC and Checkmate Press, Publishers

4364 Glenwood Dr

Bozeman, Montana 59718 USA

www.mcleanmedia.com

Hearts and Souls / Ruth Spinelli and Alean Skinner. -- 1st ed.

ISBN: 978-1-7321781-4-4

The Publisher has strived to be as accurate and complete as possible in the creation of this book.

This book is not intended for use as a source of legal, business, accounting or financial advice. All readers are advised to seek services of competent professionals in legal, business, accounting, and finance field.

In practical advice books, like anything else in life, there are no guarantees of income or results made. Readers are cautioned to rely on their own judgment about their individual circumstances to act accordingly.

While all attempts have been made to verify information provided in this publication, the Publisher assumes no responsibility for errors, omissions, or contrary interpretation of the subject matter herein. Any perceived slights of specific persons, peoples, or organizations are unintentional.

Dedication

I would like to dedicate this book to my coaches. You would be amazed at what coaches do for athletes like us. My coach drives to work and lives in another city and then comes to participate in coaching for me and the other athletes. He also likes to hunt, but instead, he will come to coach us athletes. He loves to see our team communicate and get better at the different sports we compete in for our state games.

I would also like to dedicate this book to my other coach who has always been there for me when I have needed her. She has pushed me to achieve a good time for the triathlon, which I completed all by myself this year. I actually have gotten better each year.

Finally, I would like to dedicate this to my Local Program Coordinator. She is a very awesome lady. She arranges activities for us, so we can stay busy all year long. She is the rock of our team, and without her, we wouldn't do as much as we do.

—Ruth Spinelli

I would like to dedicate this book to my family. They have supported me throughout the years when I was participating in activities away from home. And then, they became involved in Special Olympics as coaches or Unified partners.

I would like to dedicate this book to all the volunteers who have crossed my path and to those I continue to share my passion. Without these individuals, I would not have had the opportunity to be part of this wonderful organization.

I would also like to dedicate this book to all the athletes I know and to the individuals who are part of my daily life.

—Alean Skinner

Acknowledgment

We would like to thank Bob Norbie, the president of Special Olympics Montana, for helping our project get approved through the channels of Special Olympics. Thank you for your support.

We would like to thank all those who participated in filling out our surveys to get this project under way.

We would also like to thank those who encouraged us to pursue this project, which has been our dream.

Connect

Connect with the authors and learn more.

Email: heartsandsoulsofso@gmail.com

Website: https://www.heartsansouls.org

Table of Contents

Introduction

What is Special Olympics? Special Olympics is an organization for individuals with intellectual disabilities to participate year-round in sport training and competition. This book shares the ups and downs of Special Olympics. We hope those who are somehow connected to Special Olympics can find meaning in and bond with our book. We also offer this book to those who are curious about Special Olympics, so they can connect with and gain knowledge about Special Olympics and its athletes.

We gathered information by developing a simple survey for those connected to Special Olympics. The purpose of the survey is to present many, individual stories. We handed surveys out to athletes, parents, siblings, coaches/local program coordinators, volunteers, and paid employees of Special Olympics.

Our hope is for our book to generate understanding of the importance of Special Olympics. It is a peek at what Special Olympics is to those who are involved in it.

We have kept names off of the individual stories. We believe that those who filled out surveys will recognize their own story, and those who did not fill out a survey will find a connection from the stories of others.

History

Eunice Kennedy Shriver, the founder of Special Olympics, began the organization in 1968 in her back yard. Shriver spent her younger years doing sporting activities with her sister, who had an intellectual disability. She then became a college athlete and wanted to share her love of sports. She decided to start a summer sporting camp in the back of her yard for people with intellectual disabilities.

Eunice could see how the intellectually disabled were treated unfairly then, and she voiced the fact that they could do anything that they could put their minds to and that they are individuals like the rest of us.

Shriver's brother was President John F. Kennedy, in office at the same time she started the crusade to change the way individuals looked at intellectual disabilities. JFK was a stout supporter of this crusade. Today, is widespread opinion that Shriver changed the world and started a revolution surrounding the treatment of individuals with intellectual disabilities.

Eunice Kennedy Shriver wrote the oath that we still use in Special Olympics today.

"Let me win
But if I can't win
Let me be brave in the attempt."

This small summer camp, started by a thoughtful and determined woman in the 1960s, grew into the Special Olympics program you have read about in our book. Today, Special Olympics provides 32 sporting activities for individuals starting at eight years of age, with competitions ranging from the local level all the way to the international stage.

There have been many famous people that have supported Special Olympics over the years. Some of those famous people include such names as Jackie Chan, Vanessa Williams, Colin Farrell, Nelson Mandela, President Bill Clinton, Jonas Brothers, NBA, Yao Ming, and more. Jackie Chan said of Special Olympics: "I went to many countries to promote Special Olympics, through which I know there are so many misfortunes… Special Olympics may give them hope, transforming misfortunes into fortunes."

Chapter 1

Athletes

~ Ruth Spinelli

With a Chance…
I can do anything….
I can walk…
I can run….
I can Jump…
I can do all that I can and more….
I can do anything to the best of my ability with a
chance…
BY: Alean Skinner

Introduction

Special Olympics Athletes represent different lifestyles and different levels of intellectual abilities. The athletes represented in this book range in age from as young as eight years old, to those who are no longer physically able to compete in the sports programs. Some of these same athletes are in school or working every day jobs, and others who are unable to work are part of outreach services. The athletes could still be living at home, in group homes, in shared apartments, and even in their own apartments. These athletes can be anywhere from totally dependent on help to mostly independent. Some athletes needed help to fill out surveys, while others completed them out with little to no help.

The one thing they have in common is Special Olympics, offering help with exercise, friendships, and self-worth. What follows in this book are Special Olympics athletes firsthand accounts about how Special Olympics has impacted their lives, how they've grown and made new relationships through participating, and how living with a disability affects them.

Special Olympics is a completely new experience to me. It means meeting fun people and gaining a new perspective on life. It reminds me that spending time with others is what really matters. I started in high school because I had the chance to participate in a Special Education P.E. group. I really enjoyed it and got involved with Special Olympics when I moved to Bozeman. I have a few new friends that I am proud to have. I am going to graduate from college soon, and I am proud to move into the "real world." My parents have been extremely supportive in my life. They provide emotional support and support for any personal endeavors in my life. In Special Olympics, everyone is authentic and brave, an attitude that isn't found as easily outside Special Olympics. I participate in soccer and basketball, and Special Olympics has allowed me to have many friends.

Special Olympics means being supported and getting encouragement from friends and family. I started in high school. My Down syndrome makes it hard for me to speak, and it may make it harder for me to reach my goals like college. But I can do hard things; I have accomplished many things. I am a kind and friendly person. My friends trust me and enjoy my company. I graduated from high school and a year of project search training. I have worked at several jobs. I live in my own apartment with a roommate, fixing my own meals, doing my own laundry, and catching the bus to work. In high school I attended our church youth group for six years and earned a difficult award, equal to a Boy Scout Eagle Award. I also have support from my parents. I like seeing my friends, working at being healthy, and all the nice volunteers who help me and cheer for me. I love the state games and the carnival and dance. I also love the state games' health fair, traveling, and staying at a hotel. It always feels like a family reunion to see my friends each time. I participated in cycling, basketball, track and field, skiing, gymnastics and swim in the past. I also do cross-country. I have many friends and they are on my team. I started at 12 years old. I have been in Special Olympics for 13 years. Special Olympics has influenced my life for sure. I love it and it helps me stay healthy and have fun. My intellectual disability makes it hard to express my feelings and be understood.

Special Olympics means to me that we, as disability people, can be involved in sports that you feel comfortable in and where you meet new friends. I had a friend from work who encouraged me to join her team. It doesn't affect my intellectual disability. I participate in 50-meter walk, 25-meter walk, and bocce. It is hard to get 1st place in walking, but I got first in Bocce. My parents support me and also my brother and sisters support me. I love Special Olympics because I get to make new friends, travel, and also go to the dance. I do have more friends. I started Special Olympics at 40 years old. I have been in Special Olympics for three years now. Special Olympics has influenced my life by making new friends. I feel happier to have support during Special Olympics and after we go home from our meet.

Special Olympics gives me teammates and friends. I got involved with Special Olympics in Christy School. My intellectual disability makes me get confused and lost in my thoughts. I participated in basketball, bocce, swimming, and bowling. My parents do support me. I love Special Olympics because I get teammates and friends. I do have more friends. I have been with Special Olympics for 27 years. Special Olympics helped me get more friends. Having my disability, it makes it hard to independent.

Special Olympics is being good at a sport. I got started in Special Olympics in 1st grade. I got advice from my teacher that I should play soccer. I don't think that my disability will not affect me. I want to get married and be an electrician. I am high functioning autistic. I have made more friends and it made me more confident. My parents have supported me by traveling with me to State Games. I like being part of Special Olympics because I get to get out of school. I participate in basketball, cycling, running, and turbo java and have made more friends through these sports. I was six years old when I first got involved with Special Olympics and have been involved for five years now. Special Olympics has influenced my life by making more friends and also playing sports. My disability makes it difficult to talk to people.

Special Olympics means to me that I get to have friends. I started in middle school because of my teacher and mother. My intellectual disability makes me want to live my dream. Some of my accomplishments were to go to the World Games and to win lots of medals. I'm 36 years old. My parents do help me and support me.

Special Olympics is fun. I got involved with Special Olympics through the Deaf and Blind school and joined their team. My intellectual disability makes me work harder and appreciate my progress more. Some of my accomplishments are getting gold in Bocce two years in a row. I also have added three new events this year. They are snowshoeing, 25-meter walk, and also standing jump. Yes, my parents do support me but can't afford to go to the State Games. I like to compete in Special Olympics. I participate in bocce, softball throw, snowshoeing, 25-meter walk and standing broad jump. I was 12 years old when I started in Special Olympics. I have been involved with Special Olympics for 6 years. I have a few friends that I made through Special Olympics. It has made me stronger.

Special Olympics is a place to meet friends, make new friends, and be a team leader. I really don't know how I got started in Special Olympics. I love bowling and gymnastics. Special Olympics means a lot to me. It is very hard to have a goal but I just do it for fun. I participate in Bocce, gymnastics, bowling, swimming and running. My parents don't understand it.

Special Olympics is winning. I started Special Olympics in bowling. I really don't think about my intellectual disability. I participate in bowling and wheelchair racing. My parents support me in Special Olympics. I love winning in Special Olympics. I have many friends. I started Special Olympics when I was 14 years old and have been involved with Special Olympics for 35 years. Special Olympics helped me get more friends.

Special Olympics is friendships and teamwork. I joined Special Olympics when one of my parents told me that I should join. My intellectual disability makes it hard for me to get friends. I have also gotten better at running. My mother supports me in Special Olympics. I really enjoy making friends with my teammates. I participate in horseback riding and track. One of my accomplishments is that I have been able to ride on my own on a horse. I have made many friends. I was 28 years old when I started Special Olympics and I have been involved for five years. Special Olympics has influenced my life by helping me make more friends, getting more confident, and learning new skills like horseback riding. Something difficult with my intellectual disability is being an easy target for bullies. I don't like it when people laugh at me. It is difficult to do Special Olympics because I have low muscle tone.

Special Olympics means that I have fun and run races. My mother helped me sign up for Special Olympics. I have several medals and ribbons. My parents always support me. I love Special Olympics because I get to compete in bocce ball and throwing and also swimming at the hotel. I participate in races, throwing, jumping, and bocce. I have friends on my high school team. I was 10 years old when I started Special Olympics. Special Olympics has made me more confident and independent. Something that is difficult for me is accepting that I can't do everything my brothers do, like driving.

Special Olympics is having fun and meeting new people. I started Special Olympics through a friend. My life is good so far. I am able to complete my goals. I went to the 2003 World Special Olympics Games in Dublin,

Ireland and competed in soccer. I took Bronze there. My parents support me in Special Olympics. I like Special Olympics because I can make friends and compete in sports. Also, it's fun. I participate in field and track, 50-meter dash, 100-meter dash and shot put. I have many friends. I started in high school. Special Olympics helped me get back on my feet.

Special Olympics makes me realize how special I am. My parents got me involved with Special Olympics at the age of nine years old. My intellectual disability makes it hard for me to play football, but some of my accomplishments are running, bike riding, basketball and everything else. My parents do support me in Special Olympics and in real life. I love Special Olympics because I get to play basketball. I have many friends in Special Olympics. I have been involved with Special Olympics for eight years. Special Olympics influenced my life by making me learn new sports, even though it is difficult to play against strong players.

Special Olympics means helping out others and making them believe in their goals. I joined Special Olympics through my school. Some of my accomplish-ments were to help my partner achieve her goal, which was my accomplishment too. My parents are very proud of me and help me. Something that I like about Special Olympics is seeing everyone be happy about their awards. I participate in Bocce. I had friends before, but now I have made even more friends in Special Olympics. I started Special Olympics at 15 years old and have been involved for two years. Special Olympics has influenced me by helping me to appreciate every little thing in my life.

Special Olympics is a fun time for me and makes me happy. I started Special Olympics in elementary school to high school. Because of my intellectual disability, I do not plan on having a job and normal life after high school. Some of my goals and accomplishments are beating the state record in shot put and trying to improve scores every year. My parents do support me in Special Olympics. I love Special Olympics because I get to participate in my sports, opening ceremonies, and the carnival. I compete in track and field, bocce, bowling, shot put, and long jump. I have more friends in Special Olympics. I joined Special Olympics at the age of seven years old. Special Olympics has influenced my life by making me stronger, faster, more outgoing, and talkative to people.

Special Olympics is the only way I can be active. I love the friendship with other people. I got involved with Special Olympics by having some athletes come to my apartment. Some of my accomplishments are getting medals. My parents are deceased, so they don't support me. I love the ceremonies and the events that Special Olympics has offered. I participate in the individual skills basketball, track and field, walking, soft throw, and bocce. I do have friends but I don't know who they are. I began Special Olympics at age 42 years old. I have participated for nine years in Special Olympics. Special Olympics has influenced me to be more helpful and to have things under control. I have difficulty with dealing with all the pain that I have.

Special Olympics shows that people with disabilities are special too. I got started with Special Olympics because of my parent's friend. My intellectual disability affects me by not letting me play soccer because I am limited with my disability. But Special Olympics has made me get more friends and feel great about me. My parents do support me. I love Special Olympics because we all together as a big family. I participate in bocce and track. I have many friends through Special Olympics. I started at Special Olympics at the age of 24 years old. It has been my seventh year participating in Special Olympics. Special Olympics has helped me to be more positive.

Special Olympics means to me that I can play basketball and run track. And also, it also means having lots of friends. I started Special Olympics in middle school. My disability does affect me living the dream life. Some of my accomplishments are getting medals and new friends. My parents do help me. I love my team. I participate in basketball, bowling, golf and running. I have lots of friends through Special Olympics. I started Special Olympics at the age of nine years old. Special Olympics has made me happy and sociable.

Special Olympics means having friends and a vacation with my friend. I got started with Special Olympics by my wife. My disability makes me have short-term memory loss. It makes me work on remembering my friends from different towns. One of my accomplishments was getting the gold medal at the National games in 2010 for soccer. My parents do support me. I participate in basketball, floor-hockey, shot put, soccer and swimming. I have many friends through Special Olympics. I started Special Olympics at 22 years old. Special Olympics has influenced me by helping me to be always involved in something, including sports, volunteering, selling tickets and telling people about Special Olympics.

Chapter 2

Parents

~ Ruth Spinelli

My Child

My child,
I want you to have the world,
I want you to be happy,
I want you to be yourself.
My child,
There will be struggles,
There will be sadness,
There will be frustrations.
My child,
Can I see the world through your eyes?
Can I feel your happiness?
Can I let you be yourself?
You are my child forever and ever.
By: Alean Skinner

Introduction

Parents play an important role in Special Olympics. They can be their athlete's best advocates, not only in Special Olympics, but in life. Sometimes parents take on multiple roles to help provide individuals with intellectual disabilities with a chance to compete as athletes.

Parents will give countless hours looking out for special needs children to ensure they experience success and a strong sense of self-worth in their lives. Special Olympics provides for the athlete, but also allows parents to develop friendships and build a support network with other parents who understand what it's like to raise a child with a disability.

They are able to share successes and frustrations without being judged. It should also be noted that some athletes, including ones who wrote responses for this book, do not have parents that support them. Those without the support of parents and family have agencies that help them be part of Special Olympics. The Special Olympics community becomes their family.

This chapter shares the perspectives of parents of Special Olympics athletes. Learn what it's like to be a team parent and how Special Olympics has impacted the lives not just of the athletes but of their families too.

It is basically a rewarding thing to parent people with special needs. I love Special Olympics. I have seen a difference in my child by being more friendly and not feeling different from the world. I have watched my child for two years now. My best memory of my child is spending his time alone with friends and having a good time during the carnival. Some challenges for my child are a language barrier since he came from the Philippines. A highlight would be that we've both developed patience in working with this language barrier. One of his struggles is being involved in activities at school and home.

I found out about Special Olympics the previous year when my son was eight years old. I love Special Olympics because they have opportunities for people with special needs. I have watched my child for three years now. My best memory of my son was letting him have fun on his own. Some challenges for him include the fact that he is very shy and needs to be "pushed" a bit into doing events. He loves doing everything but just needs help to get started. He loves the outdoors and was central in getting a law passed so people with disabilities in Montana can hunt. One of my struggles was overcoming his shyness. I know he can do a lot of things, and truly enjoys them, if I figure out the right approach.

❖❖❖

I found out about Special Olympics from my two brothers with special needs. I have seen a difference in my child's ability to be outgoing with his friends. I watch him in three different sports. My best memory of him was going to the World Games in 1999. Some highlights of him were meeting new friends and having new friends from around the state. Some of his struggle was not having team bocce and doubles bocce and then nothing to do afterwards.

I heard about Special Olympics from my sister and her son and love it. I've seen my child change; their ability to process thoughts has increased since joining Special Olympics. I watch my athlete in all the sports. One of my favorite memories was when they ran the 400-meter all by themselves with the encouragement of the other athletes to run. They ran out of athletes to run around the track against them. A sport announcer from a Montana TV station ran with them. Some challenges are to keep them running or walking to the end of the line.

I found about Special Olympics through my school email. I love Special Olympics. I have seen a difference in my child, watching her compete in two sports. My best memory of my athlete was the joy on her face doing something she loves and is excited about. Some of their challenges are the desire to try new things she hasn't done before. I'd like to see her switch I up some. Even if she doesn't win, she doesn't seem to care. She finds more joy in just the doing and having people cheer for her to win. She struggles with a lot of things in her life that others take for granted, so it's good to see her excitement and joy about Special Olympics.

My grandson was introduced to Special Olympics in high school. I've been involved and love Special Olympics. It is a wonderful organization for special needs folks. Before Special Olympics, these folks were institutional-ized and had few life skills. It is much better now. Yes, I've seen the change in him!!! He has improved his tolerance in others, confidence in himself, and has a better sense of self-worth. I watch my child in all his sports like speed walking, bowling, soccer, basketball. One of my best memories of my athlete is seeing him smile when he is done with event.

I found out about Special Olympics while I was working at a group home in Nebraska. I like Special Olympics. I'm especially fond of the winter games. Our son has participated for several years and really feels good about doing his best. We go to all of his activities, which include basketball, track, cycling, downhill skiing, and bocce. We love seeing our son doing the 100-meter and looking up at the stand with a fist pump. He was happily in last place! It didn't matter to him, because he was doing his best. Swimming is difficult but something that he wants to do. His left hand is affected by cerebral palsy, but he wants to try it. It's always a perspective check when seeing Special Olympics doing their best with what they have been given. We've all got challenges to do our best. Honestly, our biggest struggle is getting him to practices and events. He wants to participate in everything and it takes a lot of effort to transport him.

I heard about Special Olympics on television and knew that Maria Shriver's mom started it, but didn't know much else about it. I love it; it's a wonderful program. It's very inspiring and offers so many opportunities for our daughter. Friendship and support for athletes and their families. Awesome!!!! Special Olympics keeps her active, working towards healthy goals, but also the social aspects of it make a huge difference in her life. We watch our daughter in basketball, skiing, swimming and track. In the past she competed in swimming and gymnastics. One of the greatest memories that I had with her was when she was just starting out, and we were at a swimming competition, and an adult man who was an athlete was in the pool. He had no arms but was kicking and holding up his head as he worked his way down the pool. I was so touched that I began to cry. When he reached the end of the pool, the whole place exploded in applause! Such an inspiring moment, and I will always remember that.

I found out about Special Olympics through the Bozeman Buddies group. I love Special Olympics. My child has more friends, more social engagement, is more considerate of his friends and cheers for others' successes. One of his big challenges is learning to be pushed, and being confident that he *can* do more. He enjoys belonging in the group, and every activity fun. He is so sensitive to be laughed at and bullied and doesn't tolerate teasing, even in fun. He has trouble recognizing disabilities in others and often assumes problems are his fault. We frequently have to discuss tolerance for others. Yet, the disabled aren't the only one who can't do or understand certain things. It's all of us, regardless of our ability.

I found out about Special Olympics through an elementary teacher of my oldest son. We love Special Olympics and have seen a huge difference in our son because of the program. Our Athlete participates in Soccer, track and field, swimming, floor hockey, and basketball. We watch him in every sport. One memory of our athlete was when one of our sons made the winning basket. Some challenges he faces are when other teams do not follow the rules. Some highlights are seeing my children meet and make new friends then seeing them find those same friends next time. Some struggles are having them understand certain events that happen.

I found out about Special Olympics through the schools. Yes I do love Special Olympics. I absolutely see a difference because he looks forward to it so much. He is competitive and social. I watch all of his activities. My best memory is when he was interviewed by NBC Montana in Whitefish at The Winter Games. He is in a wheelchair so sometimes he can't do what he wants and can't keep up with his peers, which is difficult for him and us.

I found out about Special Olympics when my son with autism went to Eagle Mount, and we saw that swimming pool that gets closed for Special Olympics. It's our first year with Special Olympics. We watch our son in all of his activities. And as an adult, this winter he is skiing in the advanced downhill Special Olympics even though it was his 1st year, and he was supposed to be in the intermediate. He did great in advanced group. A big part of his challenge was not being able to participate in events that he wanted to because he doesn't have teammates to participate with. The team is very small. Some of the greatest highlights were all the wonderful moments with him accomplishing his dreams and him seeing how wonderful his gift of autism is. Some struggles are that there are not many support group for autism. It would be great to have peer group meet-ups and sibling groups for those working to understand a family member with a disability.

I heard about Special Olympics through the news for years. I love Special Olympics and have seen a noticeable difference in my child with his disability. I watch my athlete in his five sports that he participates in with Special Olympics. One of my best memories was having the school come outside and cheer for our team in the games. Some challenges are the unknowns, such as trying to explain what is going to happen when they haven't experienced it before. Some highlights were the introduction to the group of people with the similar challenges. I still struggle trying to communicate with those who don't understand what it's like for someone with a disability, or for their parents.

Special Olympics has always been a well-known organization in the communities we have lived in. Participating in Special Olympics brings my child a lot of joy, and I can tell he loves playing with his teams. I watched my athlete participate in Bocce and 400-meter race and softball. My best memory is when it was my first time going to state games and supporting him. He sometimes struggles with his social skills, but he has a great personality.

I found out about Special Olympics through the school system. Since joining Special Olympics, I've seen my athlete's sense of pride in himself continue to increase. My best memory is when we saw our athlete ride in equestrian independently. Some challenges for our athlete are the times of the practices for Special Olympics and, more generally, getting services and medical care when he needs them.

We have seen a big positive change in our athlete through watching him participate in his three sports. One best memory of him is a huge smile on his face. Some challenges are the financial costs to travel and partici-pate, but we make it work. We learn something new every day through supporting our athlete and watching him grow. We work with our athlete to help him gain better understanding of others' feelings and be more accepting of his teammates and friends even when it's hard.

I found out about Special Olympics through my son's school. We do love Special Olympics — he's been doing it for 25 years now! We love watching our son compete in the state games, especially when he wins medals. He gets so excited. Some challenges are that all the activities are not in wheelchairs, so he can only participate in the ones that are wheelchair-accessible. One highlight is that he is just great at what he does.

Special Olympics is a rewarding program for the intellectually disabled. We have seen a difference in our athlete through his ability to engage in teamwork. We watch our athlete in his sports, which are Bocce, softball, and javelin. My best memory is how everyone is so happy to be an athlete. There are no challenges for our athlete. He is happy, and he likes everyone, no matter who they are. Some struggles are sometimes he is too friendly at times, and says whatever is on his mind, regardless of the situation.

I found out about Special Olympics through our family's friend. We have seen a difference in our athlete since he was in Special Olympics. We watch as many sports as he can do. It was a challenge when they wouldn't let him throw the tennis ball because he could throw it too "FAR." Some challenges are that he tries everything, so we have a lot to keep up with! Our athlete loves to have fun, so we do struggle trying to get him to stay focused and go in one direction.

I learned about Special Olympics many years ago when I was a child. I have an older sister with cerebral palsy, and she lives in a group home. She loves opening ceremonies. These activities bring joy to her life, and it's great because her nephew also participates. I love Special

Olympics very much. I get as much joy watching these athletes as they get from participating. I have seen a difference in my child very much. All human being are born with a competitive spirit, and having my son compete in Special Olympics gives him growth socially as he developed many friends through Special Olympics. My son looks forward for Special Olympics. I watch them all. I always like to be there to support him, and others that I have developed a friendship with. Each and every moment is my best memory. It's not always about winning, but about having the chance to compete and giving it your best. My son was born with low muscle tone and a cognitive delay, however, he has the heart and willingness of a champion. We all want the best for our children whether they have special needs or not. Therefore, having the opportunity to watch him grow in spirit brings joy to my heart. It's hard knowing that he has certain limitations, and trying not to baby him any different from my other child. I try my best to treat him with love and enjoy him like a child.

Chapter 3

Siblings

~ Ruth Spinelli

You and Me

You struggle differently than me,
 You see the world differently than me,
You show me your courage,
You share your happiness,
You challenge me to be more
When you work so hard for the slightest success,
I like being part of you

- Alean Skinner

Introduction

Often Special Olympics become a family affair. Not only do athletes' parents get involved, as the last chapter showed, but also quite often the siblings do too. Siblings of athletes can become Unified partners, help coach, and even help provide athlete transportation for practices and other events. Whatever their involvement, these helpful siblings are able to be part of their brother or sisters' success.

This chapter shares stories from some Special Olympics siblings, another critical part of the support that makes all this work.

I've known about Special Olympics for 15 years. I support my brother in Special Olympics. Special Olympics has been a great to help him because he is more independent. Most people aren't aware of how people with disabilities are doing high school sports. People couldn't mind their own business and always bullied those with intellectual disabilities. So I was always fighting to take a stand for him because that's not right. Something that is great about having an intellectually disabled brother is that he is the kindest hearted person I know.

I found out about Special Olympics in 2017. I do not participate in Special Olympics but I do support my sister. I feel happy that she in Special Olympics, and I've seen it change her life. Special Olympics has helped with her behavior sometimes, and she also seems to understand everything better since joining Special Olympics.

Special Olympics means everyone gets a chance to shine without being judged. Everyone can be who they are and be accepted. I got started through my school. One accomplishment was getting a blue ribbon as a unified partner. My parents are supportive because my brother is a Special Olympics athlete. I like the positive energy and seeing the smiles on the athletes' faces. I participate in Bocce as a Unified player. I have made new friends through Special Olympics too, just like the athletes do. Working with Special Olympics helps me be a more positive and happier person, constantly being surrounded by so much good energy.

Special Olympics is a place where kids can have fun and know that just because you are different does not mean that you can't do it. I got started with Special Olympics because my brother is an athlete. I'm a Unified partner. Some of my accomplishments are that

I help coach some athletes. My parents also support me in Special Olympics because my brother and I both participate. I like to play with the athletes, and I participate in bocce and golf. I was eight years old when I started with Special Olympics, and I have been in Special Olympics for two years now. Special Olympics influenced me by showing me that I can't look at people differently just because they have different abilities than me.

I found out about Special Olympics when my brother started four to five years ago. I participated as a unified player. It's a great way for him to be active, and it's also a great way for both of us to meet friends. Special Olympics has affected my life by helping me learn more about the handicapped community. My brother has mood swings, gets more attention, and it is hard for him to talk, so being part of Special Olympics is good for him.

Chapter 4

Coaches

~ Ruth Spinelli

Coaching

Communicating, teaching
Strategies, techniques
Individuals, abilities
...Coaching...
Frustrations, excitement
Fear, excitement
Losing, winning
...Coaching...
Practices, commitment
Travel, competition
Friendships forever
...Coaching...
Alean Skinner

Introduction

Coaches come from all walks of life. They are parents, family members, siblings, or volunteers. Some are passing through while others can't seem to stop.

The one thing in common is that coaching Special Olympics changes their lives in unexpected ways. They find themselves a part of an extended family with friendships that can last a lifetime.

It is not always easy to be a coach. There are communication barriers, differing athletic abilities, differing personalities, and more that a coach will learn how deal with. One thing is certain, however: once you are a coach, you will be "Coach" forever. In this chapter, Special Olympics coaches past and present reflect on what it's like to work with Special Olympic athletes.

I found out about Special Olympics through a good friend who's a participant. I do not have an athlete in Special Olympics, but I have participated as a coach for six years now. I started coaching when I went with my friend to watch him at the Winter Olympics and offered to volunteer whenever they needed me. Then I ended up coaching soccer. I love coaching because I get to spend time with all of my best friends. Absolutely every athlete player has progressed significantly in his or her own way. Coaching Special Olympics has introduced me to so many people that might have never met otherwise.

These are all profound friendships that I will maintain for the rest of my life.

I found out about Special Olympics from a friend of my mom's who is a Special Education teacher, and now I coach a team. I was a unified player (meaning I played as a teammate without a disability) for basketball for four years and have coached basketball for one year. I have coached track for three years. I got too old to be a unified player for the younger basketball team, so I decided to coach. I wanted to do another sport, so I decided to coach track. I love being around people with special needs. They are so happy and proud when they compete. Special Olympics is such a non-judgmental place. The athletes do have a lot of behavior and sportsmanship issues, but I have seen improvements over the past year. I love preparing the younger kids for high school. It has made me happier than before I became involved. There is one boy who is really special to me; we just caught each other's eye and became really close. He is a younger brother to me and I feel like I've even become part of his amazing family.

I found out about Special Olympics through my son's speech therapist. Now I have an athlete in Special Olympics and I have coached for 13 years. It came with the territory. There were many athletes to serve in my area. I like coaching because I get hugs from athletes, and because I can see my athletes succeed in their sports and watch them grow. I have seen my athletes go from running 50-meter dashes to running a mile race. Coaching has affected my life by bringing me much personal joy in seeing athletes succeed and compete. One story I have is about a young lady, 10 years old, who joined my team. She was non-verbal and very shy; she would not make any eye contact with me at all. We started with the 50-meter walk and softball throw. After two years of training hard and working with her, she has the confidence to run the 200-meter dash and uses many words to communicate with me. We both win!!!!

I found out about Special Olympics through an athlete that told me about the Kalispell Krushers after I moved into an apartment complex in Kalispell. I do not have an athlete in Special Olympics, but I have coached for five years. I volunteered at first, then they asked me if I wanted to be a coach, and now I am head coach. I get to work with a bunch of awesome athletes. They all have excelled in their sports. I've grown too. I used to be very shy and quiet, but since joining Special Olympics, I am more outgoing.

I found out about Special Olympics through a fellow teacher who ran Special Olympics in our town. I have an athlete in Special Olympics in addition to coaching, which I've done for nine years. I became a coach when the other coach retired from coaching. I love seeing the athletes compete. They look forward to this week and all year long. I look forward getting other athletes involved in outside events other than academics. I started with these kiddos in elementary school and have continued with them throughout high school. Just seeing my athletes grow year by year and watching the enjoyment they get from their accomplishments is why I coach. I am so happy to be with each athlete.

I found out about Special Olympics from my friends, family, and school. I have two girls who compete as athletes in Special Olympics, and I have coached for two years. I became a coach by signing up to be one. I love coaching because I get to see my children and friends have fun and smile when they win. I have seen much growth in my child. Coaching has affected me positively because of the joy I get seeing the athletes smile and have fun. I love being part of Special Olympics.

❖❖❖

I found out about Special Olympics when Ms. Shriver started the program. I was on the news. I do not have an athlete in Special Olympics, but I have coached for 2 months. I know an athlete who told me his team didn't have enough coaches, so I gave him my phone number for the LPC (Local Program Coordinator). Athletes are fun to be with and are so appreciative of my efforts. The biggest change I got to witness was seeing how they went from being shy or different with me to their acceptance of me. I'm retired, so it is adding to my life. I'm happy to not just be sitting at home.

I found out about Special Olympics when I went to college to be a Special Education teacher. I do not have any athletes in Special Olympics but I have coached for four years. These athletes are the most inspiring individuals I know. One young man was so excited about participating I couldn't get him to sleep. It was a long night. He went on to win an event the next day. I was very emotional.

I found out about Special Olympics in high school, 35 years ago. Now I have athlete in Special Olympics, and I have coached for 15 years. My kids did sports that I could coach, so I turned to coaching Special Olympics. It's my favorite thing other than my family. I have seen changes in my athletes every year, such as building maturity, friendships and bonds between one another. Special Olympics has changed my life by many ways that I can't even communicate. I can't image my life without Special Olympics.

I found out about Special Olympics through my school. I do have an athlete that is participating in Special Olympics, and I have coached for seven years. I volunteered and went to classes and wanted to be with my son while he was doing his sports. That's why I became a coach. I love coaching because I get to be with all the kids. Through participating in Special Olympics, my son has learned to push himself more than he used to. Coaching has helped me understand the kids better. I also love how the athletes try and never give up at what they want to do.

I found out about Special Olympics through my brother who participates in the games. I have coached for two years and I love it. My heart is full when I coach. I get great fulfillment out of it and I love to help people succeed in something they love. I wanted to be able to share what I know to the world. I coach because every year everyone seems to improve and just get a little more excited about it. These athletes show so much love and bring so much happiness. I can never stop smiling around them. I'm my brother's biggest fan and I'm his biggest fan.

I found out about Special Olympics when I was stationed at Loring Air Force Base in Maine in 1983. I received a note from my child's school saying that if parents didn't help, they wouldn't be able to have the Special Olympics games. I contacted the base commander and asked if I could be a liaison between the base and Special Olympics. I found 100 volunteers to help for the games. I do have an athlete in Special Olympics, and I have coached for 24 years. I started because my son's team needed a coach. I love being a coach because I get to see the smiles on the athletes when they compete and do well at practice and other functions. I've seen a tremendous change in their attitudes and how they progress in their sports they compete in. It has helped me have patience in dealing with all kinds of individuals. I love the joy and love the athletes that I have and their passion.

I found out about Special Olympics while working as a tutor for an 8th grader. Now, I have coached for 13 years but I got involved in Special Olympics by volunteering first. I love coaching because it gives me something to do with fabulous people. I see changes in my athletes every day. Coaching Special Olympics has made me a better person. I know someone that had extreme physical disabilities; he's shown me how to get through everything.

I have a degree in Therapeutic Recreation and I know Dr. Freeburg from Special Olympics in Illinois and Utah in the 60s. I do not have a child in Special Olympics but I have a student that is in Special Olympics, and I have coached for 20 years. I love coaching because it's a challenge. As a coach, I see so many changes in my athletes. Coaching has affected my life by learning how to be patient.

I found out about Special Olympics through another parent. I do have an athlete in Special Olympics and I have coached for three years. I became a volunteer before being a coach. I love coaching because I love to see how much these athletes can do and to watch them grow up and be confident. I have seen one athlete go from having a hard time participating, only watching from the sidelines, to now playing in his event and being much less shy.

I found out about Special Olympics through Kalispell Public Schools. They had a program that was introduced to our families. I do have an athlete who is 26 years old, a son. And I have coached for about nine years. I got involved with Special Olympics when I was asked to help with basketball skills. I enjoy the challenge of devising ways to help athletes improve their skills. I have seen athletes develop more confidence. Coaching requires a time commitment that means setting aside or delaying certain goals I've set for myself. But it's worth it. One of my favorite success stories is about one athlete who was afraid to catch a basketball. I brought a plastic ball of similar size for him to practice with, taught him to snatch balls from other players, and watched his confidence grow. His enjoyment of the game increased immensely over years.

I found out about Special Olympics because I help other special needs individuals in school. Now I have coached in Montana for 13 years. I love to coach because the athletes never cease to amaze me.

I found out about Special Olympics through another coach. I have coached for six years. I wanted to coach because I love having fun and hanging out with cool people. I have seen a difference in my athletes with their skills and their confidence. When I coach, I get excited and get energy from the athletes. I love it when the athletes get confident and gain new strengths. I am so proud of their progress.

I have known about Special Olympics since its inception. I can't remember how, but it could be because of the first U.S games were held in my hometown. Now, I have an athlete that is involved with Special Olympics and have coached for one year. The team my child belongs to needed a coach and since I was involved in organizing practices for the sport, I decided to help out. I enjoy the athletes. I like feeling I am helping the team in some way, and I enjoy seeing how much the athletes enjoy Special Olympics.

I found out about Special Olympics when I took my friend to the Winter Games and I offered to volunteer. I do not have any athletes in Special Olympics, just friends. It is my 6th year coaching. I became involved with Special Olympics by volunteering to help with the organization, and they needed a coach. It's been a great opportunity to hang out with all the friends I've made over the last six years. It's also been fun watching all our players progress in their sports. We all have gotten much more comfortable on the field. I've acquired so many new friends that I might not have met or gotten to know if it wasn't for this organization. In the six years I've been coaching, it's hard to pick just one great story about Special Olympics. Every player has the story and that's what's so amazing about Special Olympics. You develop friendships and relationships with every player and as an individual. Nobody is overlooked or left behind, and every player, regardless of skill level, is treated with respect and encouraged to do their best!

I found Special Olympics when it first arrived. Special Olympics gives individuals an opportunity to demonstrate their special talents with the encouragement of their friends and family, advocates, and the larger community. As a former worker in the human services field, in many capacities, I have several former clients participating. It's wonderful to see them shine! I have coached now for five years. The satisfaction of helping others is a good way to thrive. The realization of seeing those I've helped has helped me in return.

I found out about Special Olympics and got involved when another coach asked me to help them. I love coaching because connecting and encouraging the athletes to do well in their sports is rewarding and brings me joy. Yes, they even encourage each other when they run against each other. They show me that everyone can make a difference. One of our athletes is so sweet and encourages everyone on our team. I try to incorporate that in everyday life.

I found out about Special Olympics from my son that was in special education classes. They talked about Special Olympics in one of his classes. I have coached for 10 years and I became involved with Special Olympics because my son's team needed a coach. I love coaching because it is an opportunity to participate with my son. My teammates have made great improvement over the years.

I found out about Special Olympics through the school where I work as an aid. I have three athletes in Special Olympics, and I have coached for three years. I became a coach because the parents I work with wanted a school team. I love coaching because of the joy of the athletes, which are a blessing. A tremendous confidence has developed in one of my athletes who once was shy and afraid. Coaching has affected my life by giving me another God-Given purpose. For one of my athletes, at her 1st Special Olympics competition she was so shy that her cried every time we had her do her event. Four years later, she is excited and confident and even "hams it up"

for the fans. It's delightful to watch that kind of independence and personal growth. She has such fun, never caring what color ribbon or whether she gets a medal and will cheer for every other athlete, even those competing with her. She is an inspiring example of how to live life well.

I found out about Special Olympics from a sports coordinator from Reach. I have athletes that are participating in Special Olympics, and I have coached for two years. I love seeing the progression and happiness of the athletes and have seen much positive growth since my start with Special Olympics. Coaching has changed my life perceptive.

I found out about Special Olympics through Eagle Mount. It is my seventh year coaching. I became a coach, so I could work with my son in Special Olympics. I love coaching because it gets me on the front line. I love to cheer and also getting close with the athletes. Every year they grow stronger and better. It's been a joy and blessing. All the athletes have impressed me and impacted me so that I want to be a better person.

I found out about Special Olympics while being a volunteer instructor at Eagle Mount. I have an athlete in Special Olympics. I have coached for 10 years. I became a coach after I was a volunteer. I like to share my passion of horses and my years of experience with others.

I found out about Special Olympics when I volunteered for State Games in Asia and an individual contacted my school to start a Unified program. I have coached for two years now. I coached high school sports, and watching the games one year changed my whole outlook on sportsmanship. It makes my heart happier. My athletes have changed over the years. The athletes share with me their excitement at getting to be in an organized sport. All of my athletes did a photo shoot, and we made posters to hang up at the school. Seeing their excitement about getting to show other students their sports was so touching.

I found out about Special Olympics in high school and saw it again in college. I have no athletes of my own in Special Olympics, but I have coached for 40 years. I wanted to coach because my brother had a physical disability. I love coaching because it fills my soul with goodness. I love getting love, hugs, and happiness from Special Olympics. These athletes with physical and cognitive disabilities always work their hardest, and they never complain.

I found out about Special Olympics through my parents. At the time when I started, I had no athlete in Special Olympics. But it looks like I might have a child participating in Special Olympics when she becomes old enough. I have coached for six years now. I wanted to be a coach because I love to be a leader and wanted to help the organization. I get a lot out of Special Olympics. One of the athletes has many challenges but still maintains a smile and good spirit.

My wife has been involved with Special Olympics for years through her teaching career. I joined too, and now I have coached for seven years. A local team needed a basketball coach and I love basketball, so my wife encouraged me to help. However, basketball season is during the hunting season and I didn't want to give up the time. My wife made me, and it's maybe the best thing she ever did for me. I love the game of basketball and I love to teach. The Special Olympics athletes that I coach love to learn and love to get better. It is very rewarding to coach and watch the people you coach do their very best to implement what you are teaching. I have seen very much change in my athletes. I have watched some of them go from "I can't do that," where they didn't even want to try, to being convinced to try, to seeing them become competent at the skill with the pride that results from that. I am very appreciated by the parents and athletes for coaching the team. When co-workers or friends find out that I coach, they act like I am making a big sacrifice. It embarrasses me because I feel like I'm stealing. I get so much more out of it than I could ever give. One story I would like to share is that there is a very disabled athlete that plays basketball on a team that my team has played before. He has no use of his right side but has learned to dribble in such a way that my athletes have been unable to take the ball away from him. In our last game he made seven points, one of them being a three-pointer. It is humbling to think how hard he must have worked to become as competent as he is with the physical limitations that he possesses.

Chapter 5

Volunteers

~ Ruth Spinelli

Volunteers

Unexpected friendships,
Unexpected emotions,
Witnessing challenges,
Witnessing courage,
Unending dedication,
Unending perseverance,
This is the gold for me!
- Alean Skinner

Introduction

The role of volunteers is very important to Special Olympics. Without volunteers, area, state, national, and international games could not happen. It takes many individuals to make the games happen. We need chaperones, lunch makers, timers, coordinators for the different sites for competition, and carnival organizers. And, these are just a fraction of what is needed to help Special Olympics competition happen.

Volunteers come from all walks of life and all ages. Some help just once, and others can't seem to get enough. These volunteers, however large or small their role, are very important to Special Olympics. Read their stories about giving time with Special Olympics.

I have known about it for several years. I did not realize how much it affected the lives of the participants. A friend's son is usually very shy and while he was at the lifting competition he opened up and was having much fun. This was my first year for Special Olympics Montana. I have volunteered in archery and in races for one year, and I love the opportunity it gives to people. This provides an increase in the quality of life to many of, if not all, the Olympians. We can learn from them. The sportsmanship of the participants is on a much higher level than many of the "professional" athletes on television. I was pleasantly surprised to see how well some of the athletes performed and how much effort others put into their events. I do enjoy volunteering; it gets me out of my shell ad I get to meet people while doing it. Volunteers are a rare breed; it requires a passion for what you are volunteering for. I love archery, running, and cycling, and so I volunteer for those sports. Volunteering gives a broader perspective of the efforts that go into events like 3-D archery shoots, races, and Special Olympics. Archery club events and Special Olympics are some activities for the volunteers.

I had heard about Special Olympics before, but was approached in 2017 at my work place by Special Olympics Montana to participate in the 2018 Games when they returned to Great Falls. I have volunteered now for two years and I love everything about it. The athletes get to show off their skills that they've worked so hard on in front of their peers and in front of an audience they normally wouldn't have available. And they all look forward to the dance and carnival at the end! I learned that we can learn from them about sportsmanship, how to treat others, and about never giving up. I have learned what a positive attitude and hard work can produce by watching these athletes. If they can improve in a year since I saw them last by putting in the work, then I have absolutely no excuses. I was amazed the first year, not knowing the talent that many of the Special Olympians possess. Year one I was blown away, simply because I didn't know what to expect. This year, year two, we were even more amazed at the improvements many of the athletes had made. It was very inspiring. I love volunteering! I love getting to know these athletes. I love the inspiration they give me. I love how they humble me, and I love being a part of Special Olympics to try to give the athletes the best possible experience. They deserve that, and it can't happen without enough volunteers that care. I used to work with a gentleman that participates in SOMT. He would come into the office and shred papers or occasionally stuff envelopes for an hour a day. He was amazing to work with but I was surprised to hear he golfed and played bocce ball in the SOMT because I didn't think he had the motor skills necessary. I never would have guessed what a great golfer and bocce player he is until I went and watched him a year ago. His talent shocked me. I worked at an insurance agency and the mother of one of the athletes has insurance with us and they both come into the office frequently. He is very quiet and shy when he comes in. When I watch him at power lifting, he's totally a different person! He has confidence, he yells, and he flexes his muscles. It is amazing the transformation, and I'm not sure he would have an outlet like if it weren't for the Special Olympics.

I was in grade school and participated in the Presidential Physical Fitness test. Part of the test involved learning about the history, I learned that former President John F. Kennedy taught it many years ago, but I also learned that his sister started a program called Special Olympics that was intended to give all the athletes the opportunity to participate and excel. I thought that was pretty awesome, so many years later when given the opportunity to volunteer, I did. I still think it is awesome. I have been a volunteer since 2010 in Special Olympics. I enjoy watching the athletes compete in events they have trained and prepared for. I've learned that the only disabilities are the ones we give ourselves. I witness a determination to succeed by everyone involved. When I volunteer, I feel good inside and that I am part of a greater purpose.

When the state summer games were in Bozeman, my employer allowed us to volunteer during our first work hours. I was a volunteer in the Olympic Village and now I have volunteered for nine years. I like seeing the joy on an athlete's face when they are competing. It inspires me to be a better person and is why I continue to volunteer year after year. I've learned that our athletes have many abilities and there is no reason to focus on the disability. We need to focus on the abilities and celebrate those. Year after year I am continually amazed by what I see and what the athletes teach me. I love volunteering, especially for Special Olympics! I like to be active in the community I live in and I feel that Special Olympics does not get the attention it deserves, so I want to contribute to increase awareness. Many people are nervous to volunteer for Special Olympics because they have never been around someone with intellectual disabilities. Once they overcome being nervous, they absolutely love volunteering and come back again.

I had a friend that worked in Special Olympics Montana. It provides athletes with opportunities to focus on fitness, health, making friends, trying new things and many more opportunities. I have learned that I can learn many things from the friends I have made and athletes I watch being a part of Special Olympics. Everyone is a unique individual that brings so much to the program and I feel so blessed to have met so many wonderful people. I seek out ways to make Special Olympics a part of my life. I had to take a step back for a few years due to personal reasons/commitments and I missed it too much. I'm finally back volunteering just a bit this year and I am truly beyond excited to be involved again. I am also so excited about the Unified partner programs and how truly amazing it is so many high school kids are getting involved. I love helping others and especially supporting a program that I believe provides benefits for others in your community or world. You are truly blessed. I think volunteers really give it their best and want to make every part of Special Olympics the best it can me. I am most awe struck by parents and their level of involvement. I have met many parents that have adopted their children as well and demonstrate to me how there are so many amazing wonderful people in the world that really care and want the world to be a better place. I am generally involved at an organization level. I have been a Unified team member for spring games, the games coordinator for spring games, area director, led various area management team key areas, and been a venue leader for various sports events during spring games. I have been on the games management team for State games when they were in Bozeman, sold raffle tickets and probably a few other things. I really just like to help where the greatest need might arise so the program can continue to grow and thrive.

I had a friend who was involved with Special Olympics and got me involved. I have volunteered since 2000. Special Olympics is built around positive attitudes and supporting athletes no matter their level of ability. The program treats everyone with respect and accepts the values everyone has. Basically, these athletes are just like everyone else, but often with more joy and enthusiasm. I just feel joyful and thankful when I'm around them. They accept me as I accept them. They have giving, unselfish hearts and a respect for all the athletes without judging their level of "ability" or "disability." I have helped with paying bills, making budgets, sending thank yous, general help at the dance, area games with wheelchair events, swimming, track and field, bocce, check in, general chaperone, and whatever is needed.

I heard about Special Olympics through my school. My third-grade teacher absolutely loved getting involved. This will be my fourth year involved in Special Olympics and I am excited to volunteer for years to come! I absolutely love the enthusiasm that the athletes bring to their competitions. I am inspired by the care and compassion athletes show towards one another. Intellectual disabilities do not define a person. When volunteering, I have met some of the most influential and inspiring people I have ever had the pleasure of knowing. Every experience I have with intellectually disabled individuals is awesome. These athletes are the hardest workers and most determined doers, and love involvement and interaction. Volunteering thrills me! Having the opportunities to engage with sweet and caring people while serving as a catalyst for unity through diversity is unparalleled to other experiences. After my track team volunteers at the Special Olympics track meet, the volunteers' faces glow with concern, compassion, and joy. While many think volunteers have an impact on the athletes, the reality is the athletes have an invaluable and great impact on us. Thank you for opening our eyes to the laughter and love that exists in your world! I volunteer for Special Olympics track and field as well as Eagle mount in the wintertime preparing athletes for their Winter Games.

I heard about Special Olympics through the Hyalite Fire Department. I think it is a really cool experience for people to be able to compete and show what they've learned. I love being able to help them grow and achieve goals like this.

I first learned about Special Olympics in high school. I volunteered for a senior project and have been volunteering on and off since. I have volunteered for four years total now. I love Special Olympics! It gives the athletes a time to come together and share experiences of joy and friendship through sports. They are kind and fun people who enjoy life and being in the moment. Every year I am amazed with how great this event is and all the great outcomes from it.

My coach told me about it and that made me want to volunteer. I have volunteered for 3 years now. The community of athletes comes together for one sole purpose of life — to have fun and compete. They have determination and motivation in all of their endeavors. It is amazing how happy and supportive all the athletes are for one another, including their competitors. I am inspired every year from watching all the athletes. Most volunteers are athletes themselves. I volunteer in track races and also a lot of events.

I have learned about Special Olympics through my coaches and through the police departments. It is my second year of volunteering. I like seeing the community come together. They can do anything they put their minds to. It is inspiring. I love giving back to my community. I help out with the running events.

I found out about Special Olympics through track at my school and have volunteered for two years now. I like to help out because I feel great when they smile. I have found out that they work their hardest at the games. My school held an opening ceremony and our track was part of it, and my track coach told us we were able to help. It is a great opportunity for participants to have a chance to be like everyone else and be treated like everyone else like they should be. I have learned that these athletes are amazing people and that they can brighten anyone's day. Honestly this is all amazing and it makes me so happy that I feel like crying. I absolutely love Special Olympics. I have always felt like I had the mindset that I have had a good childhood so I should focus on helping other people.

I found out about Special Olympics through track in school. I have volunteered for one year. I love watching the athletes smile and seeing that they have fun. It is amazing because it's cool. I volunteer in cheering for the athletes.

I found out about Special Olympics through an announcement at school over the speaker. I am very new to volunteering. I love the involvement and support from the community to put on such a fun event. The athletes develop lots of confidence and are very excited to be participating in the Special Olympics. These people could not be any happier to be a part of this event. I love seeing how positive and happy the event makes people.

I found out about Special Olympics when Scott Palmer educated me on the topic. This is my rookie year. I think it's just great to get everybody out here on a nice day to compete amongst one another. They're always so happy. I think it amazing to come out and watch them enjoy their day. I enjoy in assisting our community. They are fantastic people. I volunteer in everything when it comes to Special Olympics.

I found out about Special Olympics because of an announcement at track practice. This is my first year volunteering, and I love all the athletes so much. They are so inspiring and fun to be around. I've seen how kind and sweet they are. They all provide amazing encouraging stories, and they're are all amazing and inspiring individuals. I love to help in any way that I can no matter the situation.

I found out about Special Olympics from the track coach at our school. This is my rookie year. I think it's nice to see the smiling faces after their event. I haven't learned much as of right now because this is my first year of volunteering for Special Olympics ever, but so far it has been fun. I like seeing all the smiling faces. It puts a smile on my face. I enjoy volunteering because I love helping out in our community and encouraging the people within it. I enjoy watching the youth of our community learn and grow into hardworking individuals.

I learned about Special Olympics through high school. I am a Special Education Teacher, and now I have volunteered with Special Olympics for 15 years. It brings everyone together and provides a great opportunity for athletes. There are no limits on what people can do. Everyone is so awesome and athletic! It puts positivity in my life. Unified sports rock! I volunteer in the partners club and the Unified Champion schools.

I volunteered in college with a classmate and have been involved off and on since. I have volunteered for three years with track in my area, but six or eight total in Montana and Minnesota. I love everything about Special Olympics! It's fun. The athletes just love the chance to compete and it's a good perspective for our high school athletes who volunteer to see that. In some ways, it's more fun for me to work with these athletes than with the high school team. The athletes here are pure in their approach to competing. They are happy to do their best. I love volunteering because of the unbreakable spirit of the athletes. It is one of my favorite things. It's so fulfilling. I end my day just feeling great. It's rewarding and fun. We always bring our track team and some are a little unsure of what to expect at first but some really start to love it. I had one volunteer tell me he's going to do track next year just so he can volunteer again. And I have two volunteers with our team today who didn't join track this year, but asked if they could still come with us today for the event.

I heard about Special Olympics from high school and have volunteered about one year so far. I love how it includes everyone and how the athletes have fun. Anyone can be fast no matter what obstacles come their way. I volunteer because I like to experience new things and cheer for everybody. I volunteer in the running events and love cheering.

I found out about Special Olympics through Eagle Mount. I have volunteered for one year. I think it's an excellent chance for the riders to show off their talent. I've learned that they are incredibly determined and talented. It is amazing. I love volunteering.

I heard about Special Olympics through Eagle Mount and I was asked to judge equestrian at state. I have volunteered for 36 years. I love the athletes and the 100% try you see from the athletes. They are so awesome always real and give 100%. I love it because the disabled community has taught and given me more than I ever gave them. I have learned patience and how to give my all. I volunteer because I love the athletes and they give me so much more than I can give them. They are very kind and caring people. Volunteers are from all walks of life. I volunteer for downhill skiing, cross-country and equestrian.

I heard about Special Olympics through a local team and have volunteered for five years now. I like Special Olympics because it is a connection to the community. I have learned lots through Special Olympics. Everyone is different and just because you have a disability doesn't mean you are and more different than anyone else. I am always amazed at the athletes! It certainly allows me to help others. I have learned that the volunteers have big hearts.

I heard about Special Olympics through the media and my friends. I have volunteered for one year. I love being around people who are working together and having a great time. I have learned that they are open to trying new things. I am amazed at how much community work goes into this. I volunteer because I am doing things that make people happy. Their lives are more meaningful.

I have volunteered for Special Olympics for one year. It's a great opportunity for the athletes to be with others from the state and also compete. There are wonderful people who like to have fun and experience the camaraderie. I am always amazed that the athletes are such compassionate and kind individuals. They love to get attention from one another to have fun. It makes me feel good. It gives me a sense of pride to be a part of others that make them happy. Most volunteers are in it for the same reasons as me.

I have volunteered for Special Olympics for 30 years now. I love the athletes! They are joyful and thankful. We all have strengths and weaknesses. Every year I am amazed at the athletes. It feeds my soul. Most of the volunteers are friendly and outgoing. I used to coach, but this year I am working in the games area of the Olympic Village.

I am an educator and that's how I found out about Special Olympics. This is my first year in 2018 doing Special Olympics. I like Special Olympics because of the joy on each athlete's face as well as the volunteers, including me! They are so capable. Some have more disabilities than others. They have many differences. They have both talents and disabilities. I am absolutely amazed at the athletes! I enjoy encouraging each athlete and seeing their happiness and pride at any level. They are all very caring and accepting people who enjoy diversity.

I heard about Special Olympics through work, and I have volunteered for three years. I love the athletes because they are who we should all be like. They are compassionate, supportive, loving, and accepting. They are the best to hang out with. I am amazed that more of us are not like them. I like to volunteer because I get to learn from our athletes. I volunteer wherever I am needed at the time.

I heard about Special Olympics through my mom, who works with one of the companies that makes up part of Special Olympics. It is fun to see all of the athletes get out and have fun. They are really fun to hang out with. I'm amazed at what a lot of what these people can do. I get to help and learn new things about certain disabilities. Most of the volunteers are helpful and nice.

I've known about Special Olympics from a friend at work, and I've always wanted to be involved for a very long time. I've known about Special Olympics for about 20 years. This is my first year of volunteering. I think it is a program that celebrates the uniqueness of each person. I love the way each person is a winner! Since this is my first year, I'm a learner. I am amazed at how each person is celebrated. I do like volunteering, because I believe we should give to our community. My friend and her husband volunteer each year because the Special Olympics has changed their lives.

My cousins have participated since they were young, and I have volunteered for two years. It is such an awesome thing! I love to see all these individuals come together to compete in events. They show us what happiness is, and they know how to have fun. I am absolutely amazed at these athletes. These individuals are awesome, so talented, and a joy to be around. It's so great to be part of Special Olympics. I love volunteering and it makes me happy! I volunteer in bowling, bocce ball, track and field, and basketball.

I am a Unified player and I heard about Special Olympics through a friend of the family. I have volunteered for 12 years now. I like Special Olympics because the athletes are so fun and I love helping them out. The athletes are just like everyone else. The acceptance is heartwarming. I love volunteering because it is something that keeps me happy. The athletes are Superheroes, and without them, Special Olympics would not happen. I have volunteered for track, bocce, and basketball.

I heard about Special Olympics through my cousin who has Down syndrome. I have volunteered for 33 years. I love the athletes' enthusiasm. They love everyone and seeing how much they are there for each other even if they are competing against each other is just awesome. It is rewarding to help and just see them smile, which makes me want to smile. Everyone loves to make the athletes feel loved. I volunteer as a timer at the track meets.

I used to work for Eagle Mount and one of the folks there told me about Special Olympics. This is my third year volunteering. I really enjoy working for Special Olympics. I get a chance to meet some awesome people and get out in the sun and help raise money for a special cause. I am amazed at the athletes quite a bit! I never really interacted with any folks with disabilities until I started working with Eagle Mount and then Special Olympics. I was able to start learning about adaptive sports and Special Olympics. I am amazed and the drive and vigor, and just all-around awesome sportsmanship that is always on display at the Special Olympics. It makes me glad to be a human again! I get a chance to be outside, meet great folks, and have lots of fun with good people. Volunteers are very rare breed of people who do things that make us all better.

I heard about Special Olympics through my sister's organization, which gives away t-shirts, stuffed animals, etc. Volunteers come from all walks of life and all ages. Some help once while others can't seem to get enough. These volunteers are very important to Special Olympics. I've been helping for six years. I like meeting all the different teams and seeing the enthusiasm. The athletes are such caring and sharing people. The athletes are always happy all the time when they participate. It's rewarding to be part of.

I am Para-Professional and my students participate in Special Olympics. This is my second year of volunteering. Everything is amazing; this is how the world should be! The support for the athletes is phenomenal. I love volunteering because it makes me feel all warm and fuzzy inside. They are very helpful, understanding, and compassionate.

I heard about Special Olympics through my friend that has Down syndrome. Also, I work with Autistic and special needs students in school so I was familiar with this organization. I have volunteered now for one and a half years. I love everything about Special Olympics. Looking at the world through the athletes' eyes is amazing. Everyone should get a chance to do that too. I have learned a lot. They are caring, loving and your best friends for life. They are amazing. The reason is because no matter what they always have they have a smile on their faces. I love to volunteer because it is so rewarding. I volunteer in basketball and bowling and track and field.

I heard about Special Olympics through my friends and family and have volunteered for one year. Everybody is very supportive and inclusive. It's a lot of fun and is exciting to watch. These individuals are just like me, they're strong and perseverant. The athletes are amazing because no matter what obstacles an individual faces, they overcome it with a smile on their face. I love to volunteer knowing that I helped people be happy, which makes me happy for them. Volunteers come from all over the state just to support and help out at the event. I volunteer in soccer and track and field.

Special Olympics is a good environment for everyone and a great opportunity for the athletes. I've learned that they're not much different from me, and they're very sweet and deserve to be treated with respect. It's fun to watch the athletes compete and celebrate. I like knowing I can benefit people and my community with giving just my time through volunteering. Volunteers are always helpful and come from all backgrounds which helps make Special Olympics Montana inclusive. I volunteer at soccer and track and field.

I have been aware of the games for many years. I remember when Eunice Kennedy Shriver started the first game. I have volunteered for one year for Special Olympics. I like to see the athletes having fun. That's the real reason for the games. Winning is great but participation is the best. I have learned that all people, regardless of ability, enjoy being seen and heard. The cooperation among all of the participants, parents, and coaches is very special and inspiring. It's important to give back to the community. Most volunteers believe they receive more from volunteering than they give.

I found out about Special Olympics in college as I was getting my degree in Special Education. I volunteered for two years but my job has recently interfered with that. I like Special Olympics because of its support for the community, the opportunities for athletes, and recognition of these hardworking athletes. These individuals are friendly, kind, hardworking, generous, fun, and take their sports seriously! I am amazed by the attitude and effort of the athletes. I enjoy seeing the community come together to support Special Olympics. I love volunteering because I love being around the athletes and all of the excitement! Volunteers are hardworking, dependable, king, generous, and always have fun with athletes. I volunteer in the Olympic Village and registration and as a chaperone for the athletes.

I found out about Special Olympics through a friend's child that was involved in as an athlete. I have volunteered for 1 year. I love Special Olympics because of the support for the athletes and for the mission to make events user friendly. The individuals enjoy their involvement and participation is helping one another. I am very amazed at Special Olympics and the athletes. Yes, it gives a feeling of support! Every athlete is a winner. Volunteers love seeing the enthusiasm of the athletes.

I found out about Special Olympics through school. I have volunteered for seven years. I love that it's like a second family where everyone encourages each other to do their best. I've learned how to adapt my communication skills to the needs of each athlete, and I am continuously amazed at all that these athletes can accomplish and overcome. I absolutely love volunteering. The volunteers are the greatest. I volunteer in soccer and basketball, bocce, track and field, and the winter games.

I heard about Special Olympics at my school. I have volunteered for Special Olympics for one year. I like Special Olympics because it's fun, learning about students and helping the community. There are a lot of differences among the athletes, and certain people need certain things. I love volunteering because it makes me happy to see people push themselves outside their abilities. I love helping the community. I volunteer in soccer.

Chapter 6

Employees

EMPLOYEE

organization

CEO

~ Ruth Spinelli

Special Olympics

Satisfaction	**O**bstacles
Perfect	**L**iving
Energy	**Y**ears
Courageous	**M**emorable
Individuals	**P**erseverance
Activities	**I**nfectious
Loving	**C**ommunity
Success	

- Ruth Spinelli and Alean Skinner

Introduction

Those who have chosen to work for Special Olympics have a passion to work with people. They are dedicated individuals and provide a wonderful service, including helping raise funds, finding volunteers, encouraging individuals with intellectual disabilities to become part of this organization, and more. Without these individuals there would not be Special Olympics.

This chapter shares insights from Special Olympics employees on what it's like to work for the organization, as well as the impact the organization has had on their own lives and the lives of others.

I have a passion to work with people. A few of my top strengths include positivity and harmony, both of which I believe Special Olympics athletes portray on a daily basis. It felt like a great opportunity to be employed by an organization with a strong mission that I can truly relate to. In high school I sang in choir. I recall my first experience with Special Olympics when our choir sang at opening ceremonies for state summer games. To my recall, the first contact that I truly had besides passing individuals in town or in school was then I began working at Special Olympics Montana. The athletes are absolutely amazing. Working with these individuals makes me strive to stay positive in my outlook, due to the fact that many of our athletes are facing bigger issues. I have been an employee at Special Olympics Montana for almost four years now. One of the greatest challenges is simply seeing the lack of education for community members when working with individuals with intellectual disabilities. It's a struggle to help everyone learn that we are all much more alike than different and we do not need to fear "different." Every day is truly a success with Special Olympics. Some days may be harder than others, but seeing the smiles on our athletes' faces at events when they receive a medal or even a participation ribbon — the joy they get makes everything worth it.

The organization is amazing and does so much for the community. I love that I get to spend time working for a cause that makes a difference. My uncle has Down syndrome so I have been involved with Special Olympics my whole life. I loved watching him bowl and was so proud of him for all his hard work. I would not be the person I am without the influence of my uncle and his friends, teammates, and coworkers with disabilities. My involvement with them has made me a more empathetic and passionate person. I have been employed with Special Olympics Montana for three years now. One of my biggest challenges is the ability to have a work/life balance. Special Olympics is such a good cause that it can be hard not to work nonstop to achieve our goals. A major success I've seen is spreading our mission of inclusion and respect.

I chose to work for Special Olympics Montana because I have a desire to serve and to have fun. I was 18 years old when I started at Eagle Mount. My first contact with Special Olympics was in 1960 in grade school. This ongoing relationship with people with intellectual disabilities has forever enriched my life.

I believe that strong communities are those that include their members with intellectual disabilities to be their true and full selves. My first contact with an intellectually disabled individual was in elementary school. Since then, my life has been influenced day in and day out. I watch individuals with intellectual disabilities model the athlete oath, "Let me win. But if I can't win, let me brave in the attempt." On a daily basis, Special Olympics athletes inspire me to live life fully. I have served as the Chief Operating Officer of Special Olympics Montana for nearly five years. As employees, we struggle with too little time to complete work that would advance the Special Olympics mission.

Why did I choose to be employed by Special Olympics Montana? Perhaps it was just blind luck. Some years back I determined that I wasn't interested in building widgets with my business degree. Instead, I wanted to build lives. This passion took me to outdoor adventure-based programs for about 15 years before learning about an opportunity with Special Olympics Montana through a colleague. While living in Florida at the time, directing a program for Hurricane Island Outward Bound School, I applied for the Special Olympics Montana President/CEO (then Executive Director) position. That was 26 years ago. And, as they say, the rest is history. My first experience with Special Olympics was my first day on the job with Special Olympics Montana. My first memorable contact with athletes was during the 1993 CM Russell Area Basketball Tournament hosted at the Montana School for the Deaf & Blind in Great Falls with my then very young children, Kirsten and Erik. The athletes' enthusiasm and intensity to play ball and do their best was captivating. I met many athletes and from that moment, began creating many new friendships. I did not have any immediate family member with intellectual disabilities. This said, I had worked and played with different ability people as a college student through our outdoor adventure club and instructed different groups of people (i.e. children, minority groups, those with physical disabilities, juvenile delinquents, adults in transition, etc.) through my experiences with Outward Bound.

My immersion really began when I became the CEO of Special Olympics Montana the winter of 1993. My life and the lives of my family have been influenced considerably by the athletes we serve. Athletes are masterful teachers if we pause long enough to listen. They inherently understand the difference between "North" and "True North." By their words and actions, athletes have guided me to be the best me possible. By their words and actions, athletes have modeled a credo that I developed and shared with my children at a young age: "Be good. Do good. Never give up." For all those 26 years that I've been employed by Special Olympics Montana, I've served as the President and Chief Executive Officer. Even when I retire from this role, I expect to remain a fan and volunteer for a lifetime. Perhaps the single biggest struggle has to do with attitudes. People stereotype and pigeon-hole those people and things they don't understand or fear. It takes considerable effort to overcome attitudes that marginalize, minimize, ostracize, and bully others. Indeed, the most pervasive disability we, as a society, have is our attitudes. Specific to Special Olympics Montana, our single biggest challenge is to have enough capacity to serve many more eligible athletes who are sitting on the sidelines just waiting for a chance to train for life through sports and become all they can be. In Special Olympics terms, "lack of capacity" refers to the need for more fans and funds. Or more bluntly, more volunteers and money. On a statewide level, right now we have nearly 3,000 successes annually. Those successes are the athletes we serve, both athletes with intellectual disabilities and Unified teammates. Specific to any one athlete, there are countless stories to share. One comes from a Missoula athlete some years ago when she ran up to me at a State Summer Games Dance Carnival and said, "I feel really good about myself." When I said, "why is that?" she said, "Because everyone here treats me the way I want to be." That is simply profound. Simply profound because that's what we all want. To be treated the way we want to be treated. This said, organizationally and programmatically, SOMT has accomplished much over the years. From once when we were only a traditional Special Olympics program with sports our singular focus, today our platform is much more expansive and inclusive. A tremendous effort goes into our Unified Champions School program that emphasizes Unified Sports, Youth Leadership and Whole School involvement. We have an integrated Healthy Athlete/Healthy Communities program. We have a focus on our indigenous population and are currently piloting efforts on the Flathead Reservation. We are now a movement that integrates sports, health, education and community-building initiatives to transform lives and create communities of acceptance, respect and inclusion.

Conclusion

A reoccurring theme throughout the chapters is that Special Olympics have a profound effect on anyone who is involved with this program. We believe that positive impact contributes to the success of Special Olympics.

Volunteers, parents, siblings, and employees all love seeing the success of these athletes. They can see them grow. They can see them be part of something that has no judgment. And they make lots of friends, who have become an extended family. These individuals witness the joy, the success, and the confidence the athletes have developed because of fitting into the world through sports competition. Many of these individuals volunteer repeatedly.

Perhaps most importantly, the recurring impacts we see throughout the athletes' entries include confidence, long-lasting friendships, extended families, involvement, and more. We believe that Special Olympics enriches the individual athletes' lives as well as those of the community that surrounds our athletes.

The Authors' Stories

My name is Ruth Spinelli and I am 38 years old. I was born in Falls Church, Virginia. I went to school in Virginia and received my diploma from Falls Church High School.

After high school, I attended Kings College in Wilkes-Barre Pennsylvania where they were able to provide services I needed for one semester. I played field hockey and Lacrosse while I was there. I did not do so well in a four- year college so I went back to Virginia to go to a 2-year college.

My family then decided to move to Montana after many years of living and working in Virginia. I have been in Bozeman since 2014.

My first time trying to get involved in Special Olympics was in Virginia, but I was unable to make contact with the organization.

However, once in Montana my brother told me about the Special Olympic programs. My brother's wife knew about Eagle Mount and suggested talking to them to see how to get involved with Special Olympics. They suggested starting with a basketball team. I found a team that had room for me and became part of the Bozeman Flames.

I have been part of the Flames since 2014. With the Flames I have tried more sports such as horseback riding. It turns out I love horseback riding. Some of the other sports I do include basketball, skiing, long jump, 1500 run, and few others. I participate in sports year around.

There were some sports that I had no idea of what they were. I had to learn about those sports. I will never leave Special Olympics.

Special Olympics is more than sports too. I had an opportunity to become a Global Messenger. As a global messenger, I am able to talk to companies or other parties. I talk to them about Special Olympics' and what we need from them such as volunteers or donations. Being a Global Messenger is awesome!

I have a volunteer that is 80 years old and I had a goal to ski in areas with the black markers at Bridger Bowl. The black markers are where the highest point of the mountain. He actually helped me achieve that goal. We also went skydiving together for his 80th birthday. It is a good thing that we have volunteers that will help individuals with intellectual disabilities accomplish goals.

Another one of my goals in life is to graduate from college. Reading and comprehension is hard for me. I am still hope to achieve this goal.

I want you to know Special Olympics has made most of my goals come true for me. I can actually be myself and be active in sports. Another good thing about being involved with Special Olympics is you are always busy because it's all year long.

Having a disability makes it harder to accomplish the dreams that I have for my life. One of my dreams is to write a book and be a Pro Athlete. Hopefully, one of my dreams will come true someday as I am in the process of writing a book with my Global Messengers coach.

Special Olympics means a lot to me. It's about having a bigger family, friends and something to be involved with these days. It also helps me keep in shape and be active during the other hours of the day year around.

My name is Alean Skinner. I am a retired Special Education teacher. I have been involved with Special Olympics for many years. My involvement began as a volunteer for the carnival during state games. Later I became a coach and then became part of the Area Management Team. Now a days I help coach a team, remain part of the AMT as an ALP's coordinator, (training athletes to be Global Messengers), and whatever else is needed.

My life has been enriched by being part of Special Olympics. I have lifelong friends with a group of individuals who are non-judgmental.

There are times these activities are exhausting and even frustrating. Sometimes helping can feel more like a fulltime job but it hasn't been enough to stop me from going back for more.

Sometimes the athletes can be hard until you learn what makes them tick and then you have a friend for life.

I am fortunate also that my family is involved as well. My husband and daughter are coaches. My son-in-law is a unified partner. And in the future, I will have a grand-daughter who will become a Special Olympic athlete.

I am fortunate to have many athletes part of my daily life. I know how their jobs are going, how school is going, and any other thing they want to share. I am flattered to be considered a good friend. I even get to go to celebrations, movies, cookie making and more.

For now, I couldn't think of anything better than being involved with Special Olympics. And I love that my family is part of it. We are together and part of something great.

Survey Questions Used

NO NAMES, phone numbers or Address. Special Olympics book for Athletes

This survey is completely voluntary and anonymous. We are gathering information to write a book about Special Olympics. Your help will be greatly appreciated. What does Special Olympics mean to you? How did you start getting involved with SO? How does your intellectual disability affect your life and goals? What are some of your accomplishments? Did your parents support you? Tell me something you like about Special Olympics? What sports do you participate in? Do you have many friends now and does SO have something to do with that? How old were you when you started Special Olympics? How long in Special Olympics? How has SO influenced your life? Tell something that is hard about having an intellectual disability?

Survey for Coaches

How did you find out about SO? Do you have an athlete that is participating in SO? How many years have you coached? What made you want to be a coach? Why do you like doing it? Have you seen much change in athletes? Do you get anything out of the athletes? Tell us a story about an athlete that you look up too? (DO not use names)

Survey for Volunteers

How did you hear about Special Olympics? How many years have you volunteered? Do you love Special Olympics? Why? Have you learned anything about intellectual disabled individuals? Are you amazed at what you learn or see? Why??? Do you love volunteering? Why Tell an interesting fact about volunteers that you may know? What activity or activities do you volunteer for?

Parenting Survey

How did you find out about Special Olympics? Do you like Special Olympics? Do you see a difference in your child/athlete? How many activities do you watch your athlete in? What is your best memory? What are some challenges for your athlete related to Special Olympics? What are some highlights with having a child with intellectual disability? What are some struggles with having a child with intellectual disabilities?

Employed for Special Olympics

Why did you choose to be employed with SO? What was your first experience with SO? When was your first contact with an intellectual disabled individual? Has your life been influenced by individuals with intellectual disabilities? How? How? long have you been part of SO has an employee? How long in any other capacity? Tell about a struggle with SO? Tell about a success with SO?

References

Xinh 2007-10-02 Jackie Chan: Special Olympics Gives hope to Parents of Mentally Challenged. Retrieved from
http://english.cri.cn/2886/2007/10/02/1681@280269.

Kennedy Jr., Joseph Foundation (Perfect Sense) About Eunice Kennedy Shriver

Retrieved from www.specialolympics.org

Connect

Connect with the authors and learn more.

Email: heartsandsoulsofso@gmail.com

Website: https://www.heartsansouls.org

Made in USA - Kendallville, IN
83248_9781732178144
11.10.2021 1609